HAL•LEONARD
INSTRUMENTAL
PLAY-ALONG

AUDIO
ACCESS
INCLUDED

PLAYBACK+
Speed • Pitch • Balance • Loop

VIOLA

PIRATES OF THE CARIBBEAN

T0081551

To access audio visit:
www.halleonard.com/mylibrary

5175-6486-3415-1331

ISBN 978-1-4234-2203-7

Disney characters and artwork © Disney Enterprises, Inc.

WALT DISNEY MUSIC COMPANY

DISTRIBUTED BY

HAL•LEONARD®
CORPORATION

7777 W. BLUEMOUND RD. P.O. BOX 13819 MILWAUKEE, WI 53213

For all works contained herein:
Unauthorized copying, arranging, adapting, recording or public performance is an infringement of copyright.
Infringers are liable under the law.

Visit Hal Leonard Online at
www.halleonard.com

Title	Page

THE BLACK PEARL

VIOLA

Music by KLAUS BADELT

© 2003 Walt Disney Music Company
All Rights Reserved   Used by Permission

5

BLOOD RITUAL/
MOONLIGHT SERENADE

VIOLA

Music by KLAUS BADELT

© 2003 Walt Disney Music Company
All Rights Reserved   Used by Permission

DAVY JONES PLAYS HIS ORGAN

VIOLA

Music by HANS ZIMMER

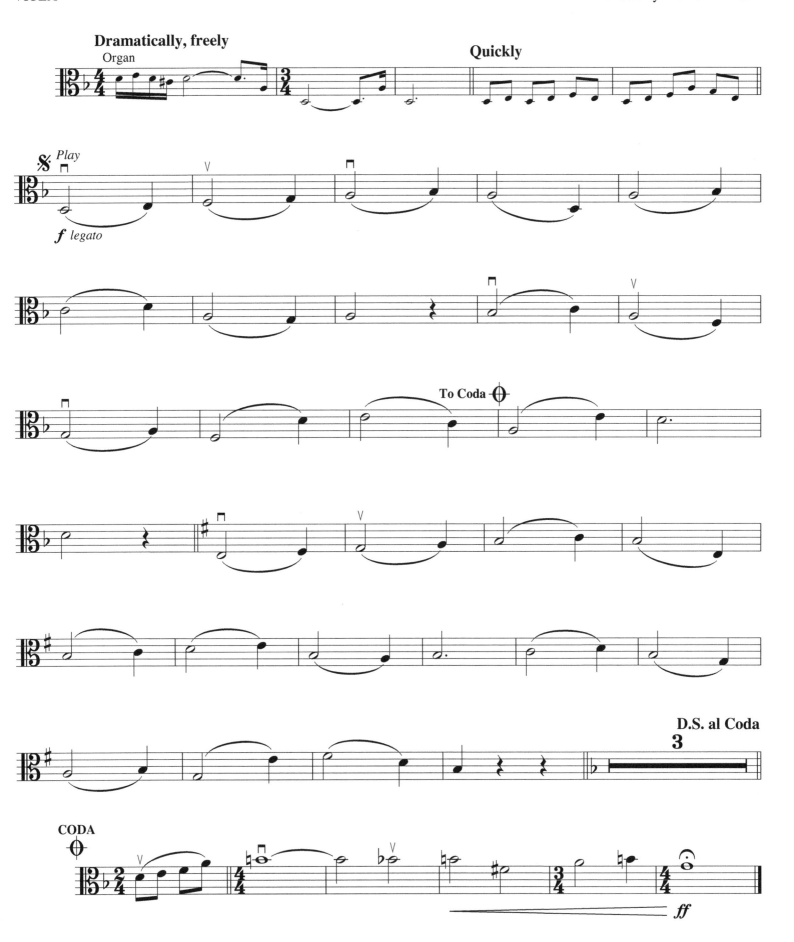

© 2006 Walt Disney Music Company
All Rights Reserved   Used by Permission

DAVY JONES

VIOLA

Music by HANS ZIMMER

© 2006 Walt Disney Music Company
All Rights Reserved   Used by Permission

DINNER IS SERVED

VIOLA

Music by HANS ZIMMER

© 2006 Walt Disney Music Company
All Rights Reserved   Used by Permission

I'VE GOT MY EYE ON YOU

VIOLA

Music by HANS ZIMMER

© 2006 Walt Disney Music Company
All Rights Reserved Used by Permission

HE'S A PIRATE

VIOLA

Music by KLAUS BADELT

© 2003 Walt Disney Music Company
All Rights Reserved   Used by Permission

JACK SPARROW

VIOLA

Music by HANS ZIMMER

© 2006 Walt Disney Music Company
All Rights Reserved Used by Permission

THE KRAKEN

VIOLA

Music by HANS ZIMMER

Slow and steady

© 2006 Walt Disney Music Company
All Rights Reserved   Used by Permission

THE MEDALLION CALLS

VIOLA

Music by KLAUS BADELT

© 2003 Walt Disney Music Company
All Rights Reserved   Used by Permission

ONE LAST SHOT

VIOLA

Music by KLAUS BADELT

© 2003 Walt Disney Music Company
All Rights Reserved Used by Permission

TO THE PIRATE'S CAVE!

VIOLA

Music by KLAUS BADELT

© 2003 Walt Disney Music Company
All Rights Reserved   Used by Permission

TWO HORNPIPES
(Fisher's Hornpipe)

VIOLA

By SKIP HENDERSON

Copyright © 1997 by Skip Henderson
All Rights Reserved   Used by Permission

WHEEL OF FORTUNE

VIOLA

Music by HANS ZIMMER

© 2006 Walt Disney Music Company
All Rights Reserved   Used by Permission

UNDERWATER MARCH

VIOLA

Music by KLAUS BADELT

© 2003 Walt Disney Music Company
All Rights Reserved   Used by Permission